The Constitution of the
State of Wisconsin:
A Quick Reference Guide

Bootblack Budget Books
Copyright 2018 ©
ISBN-13: 978-1726472739
ISBN-10: 1726472736

Contents:

Preamble – Page 19

Article I: Declaration of Rights – Page 20

Section 1. Equality; Inherent Rights

Section 2. Slavery Prohibited

Section 3. Free Speech; Libel

Section 4. Right to Assemble and Petition

Section 5. Trial by Jury; Verdict in Civil Cases

Section 6. Excessive Bail; Cruel Punishments

Section 7. Rights of Accused

Section 8. Prosecutions; Double Jeopardy; Self-Incrimination; Bail; Habeas Corpus

Section 9. Remedy for Wrongs

Section 9m. Victims of Crime

Section 10. Treason

Section 11. Searches and Seizures

Section 12. Attainder; Ex Post Facto; Contracts

Section 13. Private Property for Public Use

Section 14. Feudal Tenures; Leases; Alienation

Section 15. Equal Property Rights for Aliens and Citizens

Section 16. Imprisonment for Debt

Section 17. Exemption of Property of Debtors

Section 18. Freedom of Worship; Liberty of Conscience; State Religion; Public Funds

Section 19. Religious Tests Prohibited

Section 20. Military Subordinate to Civil Power

Section 21. Rights of Suitors

Section 22. Maintenance of Free Government

Section 23. Transportation of School Children

Section 24. Use of School Buildings

Section 25. Right to Keep and Bear Arms

Section 26. Right to Fish, Hunt, Trap, and Take Game

Article II: Boundaries – Page 28

Section 1. State Boundary

Section 2. Enabling Act Accepted

Article III: Suffrage – Page 30

Section 1. Electors

Section 2. Implementation

Section 3. Secret Ballot

Section 4. Repealed

Section 5. Repealed

Section 6. Repealed

Article IV: Legislative – Page 32

Section 1. Legislative Power

Section 2. Legislature, How Constituted

Section 3. Apportionment

Section 4. Representatives to the Assembly, How Chosen

Section 5. Senators, How Chosen

Section 6. Qualifications of Legislators

Section 7. Organization of Legislature; Quorum; Compulsory Attendance

Section 8. Rules; Contempts; Expulsion

Section 9. Officers

Section 10. Journals; Open Doors; Adjournments

Section 11. Meeting of Legislature

Section 12. Ineligibility of Legislators to Office

Section 13. Ineligibility of Federal Officers

Section 14. Filling Vacancies

Section 15. Exemption From Arrest and Civil Process

Section 16. Privilege in Debate

Section 17. Enactment of Laws

Section 18. Title of Private Bills

Section 19. Origin of Bills

Section 20. Yeas and Nays

Section 21. Repealed

Section 22. Powers of County Boards

Section 23. Town and County Government

Section 23a. Chief Executive Officer to Approve or Veto Resolutions or Ordinances; Proceedings on Veto.

Section 24. Gambling

Section 25. Stationery and Printing

Section 26. Extra Compensation; Salary Change

Section 27. Suits Against State

Section 28. Oath of Office

Section 29. Militia

Section 30. Elections by Legislature

Section 31. Special and Private Laws Prohibited

Section 32. General Laws on Enumerated Subjects

Section 33. Auditing of State Accounts

Section 34. Continuity of Civil Government

Article V: Executive – Page 45

Section 1. Governor; Lieutenant Governor; Term

Section 1m. Repealed

Section 1n. Repealed

Section 2. Eligibility

Section 3. Election

Section 4. Powers and Duties

Section 5. Repealed

Section 6. Pardoning Power

Section 7. Lieutenant Governor, When Governor

Section 8. Secretary of State, When Governor

Section 9. Repealed

Section 10. Governor to Approve or Veto Bills; Proceedings on Veto

Article VI: Administrative – Page 50

Section 1. Election of Secretary of State, Treasurer and Attorney General; Term

Section 1m. Repealed

Section 1n. Repealed

Section 1p. Repealed

Section 2. Secretary of State; Duties, Compensation

Section 3. Treasurer and Attorney General; Duties, Compensation

Section 4. County Officers; Election, Terms, Removal; Vacancies

Article VII: Judiciary – Page 53

Section 1. Impeachment; Trial

Section 2. Court System

Section 3. Supreme Court: Jurisdiction

Section 4. Supreme Court: Election, Chief Justice, Court System Administration

Section 5. Court of Appeals

Section 6. Circuit Court: Boundaries

Section 7. Circuit Court: Election

Section 8. Circuit Court: Jurisdiction

Section 9. Judicial Elections, Vacancies

Section 10. Judges: Eligibility to Office

Section 11. Disciplinary Proceedings

Section 12. Clerks of Circuit and Supreme Courts

Section 13. Justices and Judges: Removal by Address

Section 14. Municipal Court

Section 15. Repealed

Section 16. Repealed

Section 17. Repealed

Section 18. Repealed

Section 19. Repealed

Section 20. Repealed

Section 21. Repealed

Section 22. Repealed

Section 23. Repealed

Section 24. Justices and Judges: Eligibility for Office; Retirement

Article VIII: Finance – Page 60

Section 1. Rule of Taxation Uniform; Income, Privilege and Occupation Taxes

Section 2. Appropriation; Limitation

Section 3. Credit of State

Section 4. Contracting State Debts

Section 5. Annual Tax Levy to Equal Expenses

Section 6. Public Debt for Extraordinary Expense; Taxation

Section 7. Public Debt for Public Defense; Bonding for Public Purposes

Section 8. Vote on Fiscal Bills; Quorum

Section 9. Evidences of Public Debt

Section 10. Internal Improvements

Section 11. Transportation Fund

Article IX: Eminent Domain and Property of the State – Page 67

Section 1. Jurisdiction on Rivers and Lakes; Navigable Waters

Section 2. Territorial Property

Section 3. Ultimate Property in Lands; Escheats

Article X: Education – Page 68

Section 1. Superintendent of Public Instruction

Section 2. School Fund Created; Income Applied

Section 3. District Schools; Tuition; Sectarian Instruction; Released Time

Section 4. Annual School Tax

Section 5. Income of School Fund

Section 6. State University; Support

Section 7. Commissioners of Public Lands

Section 8. Sale of Public Lands

Article XI: Corporations – Page 71

Section 1. Corporations; How Formed

Section 3. Municipal Home Rule; Debt Limit; Tax to Pay Debt

Section 3a. Acquisition of Lands By State and Subdivisions; Sale of Excess

Section 4. General Banking Law

Section 5. Repealed

Article XII: Amendments – Page 74

Section 1. Constitutional Amendments

Section 2. Constitutional Conventions

Article XIII: Miscellaneous Provisions – Page 75

Section 1. Political Year; Elections

Section 2. Repealed

Section 3. Eligibility to Office

Section 4. Great Seal

Section 5. Repealed

Section 6. Legislative Officers

Section 7. Division of Counties

Section 8. Removal of County Seats

Section 9. Election or Appointment of Statutory Officers

Section 10. Vacancies in Office

Section 11. Passes, Franks and Privileges

Section 12. Recall of Elective Officers

Section 13. Marriage

Article XIV: Schedule – Page 80

Section 1. Effect of Change from Territory to State

Section 2. Territorial Laws Continued

Section 3. Repealed

Section 4. Repealed

Section 5. Repealed

Section 6. Repealed

Section 7. Repealed

Section 8. Repealed

Section 9. Repealed

Section 10. Repealed

Section 11. Repealed

Section 12. Repealed

Section 13. Common Law Continued in Force

Section 14. Repealed

Section 15. Repealed

Section 16. Implementing Revised Structure of Judicial Branch

PREAMBLE

We, the people of Wisconsin, grateful to Almighty God for our freedom, in order to secure its blessings, form a more perfect government, insure domestic tranquility and promote the general welfare, do establish this constitution.

ARTICLE I: DECLARATION OF RIGHTS

Section 1. Equality; Inherent Rights

All people are born equally free and independent, and have certain inherent rights; among these are life, liberty and the pursuit of happiness; to secure these rights, governments are instituted, deriving their just powers from the consent of the governed.

Section 2. Slavery Prohibited

There shall be neither slavery, nor involuntary servitude in this state, otherwise than for the punishment of crime, whereof the party shall have been duly convicted.

Section 3. Free Speech; Libel

Every person may freely speak, write and publish his sentiments on all subjects, being responsible for the abuse of that right, and no laws shall be passed to restrain or abridge the liberty of speech or of the press. In all criminal prosecutions or indictments for libel, the truth may be given in evidence, and if it appears to the jury that the matter charged as libelous be true, and was published with good motives and for justifiable ends, the party shall be acquitted; and the jury shall have the right to determine the law and fact.

Section 4. Right to Assemble and Petition

The right of the people peaceably to assemble, to consult for the common good, and to petition the government, or any department thereof, shall never be abridged.

Section 5. Trial by Jury; Verdict in Civil Cases

The right of trial by jury shall remain inviolate, and shall extend to all cases at law without regard to the amount in controversy; but a jury trial may be waived by the parties in all cases in the manner prescribed by law. Provided, however, that the legislature may, from time to time, by statute provide that a valid verdict, in civil cases, may be based on the votes of a specified number of the jury, not less than five-sixths thereof.

Section 6. Excessive Bail; Cruel Punishments

Excessive bail shall not be required, nor shall excessive fines be imposed, nor cruel and unusual punishments inflicted.

Section 7. Rights of Accused

In all criminal prosecutions the accused shall enjoy the right to be heard by himself and counsel; to demand the nature and cause of the accusation against him; to meet the witnesses face to face; to have compulsory process to compel the attendance of witnesses in his behalf-, and in prosecutions by indictment, or information, to a speedy public trial by an impartial jury of the county or district wherein the offense shall have been committed; which county or district shall have been previously ascertained by law.

Section 8. Prosecutions; Double Jeopardy; Self-Incrimination; Bail; Habeas Corpus

(1) No person may be held to answer for a criminal offense without due process of law, and no person for the same offense may be put twice in jeopardy of punishment, nor may be compelled in any criminal case to be a witness against himself or herself.

(2) All persons, before conviction, shall be eligible for release under reasonable conditions designed to assure their appearance in court, protect members of the community from serious bodily harm or prevent the intimidation of witnesses. Monetary conditions of release may be imposed at or after the initial appearance only upon a finding that there is a reasonable basis to believe that the conditions are necessary to assure appearance in court. The legislature may authorize, by law, courts to revoke a person's release for a violation of a condition of release.

(3) The legislature may by law authorize, but may not require, circuit courts to deny release for a period not to exceed 10 days prior to the hearing required under this subsection to a person who is accused of committing a murder punishable by life imprisonment or a sexual assault punishable by a maximum imprisonment of 20 years, or who is accused of committing or attempting to commit a felony involving serious bodily harm to another or the threat of serious bodily harm to another and who has a previous conviction for committing or attempting to commit a felony involving serious bodily harm to another or the threat of serious bodily harm to another. The legislature may authorize by law, but may not require, circuit courts to continue to deny release to those accused persons for an additional period not to exceed 60 days following the hearing required under this subsection, if there is a requirement that there be a finding by the court based on clear and convincing evidence presented at a hearing that the accused committed the felony and a requirement that there be a finding by the court that available conditions of release will not adequately protect members of the community from serious bodily harm or prevent intimidation of witnesses. Any law enacted under this subsection shall be specific, limited and reasonable. In determining the 10-day and 60-day periods, the court shall omit any period of time found by the court to result from a delay caused by the defendant or a continuance granted which was initiated by the defendant.

(4) The privilege of the writ of habeas corpus shall not be suspended unless, in cases of rebellion or invasion, the public safety requires it.

Section 9. Remedy for Wrongs

Every person is entitled to a certain remedy in the laws for all injuries, or wrongs which he may receive in his person, property, or character; he ought to obtain justice freely, and without being obliged to purchase it, completely and without denial, promptly and without delay, conformably to the laws.

Section 9m. Victims of Crime

This state shall treat crime victims, as defined by law, with fairness, dignity and respect for their privacy. This state shall ensure that crime victims have all of the following privileges and protections as provided by law: timely disposition of the case; the opportunity to attend court proceedings unless the trial court finds sequestration is necessary to a fair trial for the defendant; reasonable protection from the accused throughout the criminal justice process; notification of court proceedings; the opportunity to confer with the prosecution; the opportunity to make a statement to the court at disposition; restitution; compensation; and information about the outcome of the case and the release of the accused. The legislature shall provide remedies for the violation of this section. Nothing in this section, or in any statute enacted pursuant to this section, shall limit any right of the accused which may be provided by law.

Section 10. Treason

Treason against the state shall consist only in levying war against the same, or in adhering to its enemies, giving them aid and comfort. No person shall be convicted of treason unless on the testimony of two witnesses to the same overt act, or on confession in open court.

Section 11. Searches and Seizures

The right of the people to be secure in their persons, houses, papers, and effects against unreasonable searches and seizures shall not be violated; and no warrant shall issue but upon probable cause, supported by oath or affirmation, and particularly describing the place to be searched and the persons or things to be seized.

Section 12. Attainder; Ex Post Facto; Contracts

No bill of attainder, ex post facto law, nor any law impairing the obligation of contracts, shall ever be passed, and no conviction shall work corruption of blood or forfeiture of estate. Private property for public use.

Section 13. Private Property for Public Use

The property of no person shall be taken for public use without just compensation therefore.

Section 14. Feudal Tenures; Leases; Alienation

All lands within the state are declared to be allodial, and feudal tenures are prohibited. Leases and grants of agricultural land for a longer term than fifteen years in which rent or service of any kind shall be reserved, and all fines and like restraints upon alienation reserved in any grant of land, hereafter made, are declared to be void.

Section 15. Equal Property Rights for Aliens and Citizens

No distinction shall ever be made by law between resident aliens and citizens, in reference to the possession, enjoyment or descent of property.

Section 16. Imprisonment for Debt

No person shall be imprisoned for debt arising out of or founded on a contract, expressed or implied.

Section 17. Exemption of Property of Debtors

The privilege of the debtor to enjoy the necessary comforts of life shall be recognized by wholesome laws, exempting a reasonable amount of property from seizure or sale for the payment of any debt or liability hereafter contracted.

Section 18. Freedom of Worship; Liberty of Conscience; State Religion; Public Funds

The right of every person to worship Almighty God according to the dictates of conscience shall never be infringed; nor shall any person be compelled to attend, erect or support any place of worship, or to maintain any ministry, without consent; nor shall any control of, or interference with, the rights of conscience be permitted, or any preference be given by law to any religious establishments or modes of worship; nor shall any money be drawn from the treasury for the benefit of religious societies, or religious or theological seminaries.

Section 19. Religious Tests Prohibited

No religious tests shall ever be required as a qualification for any office of public trust under the state, and no person shall be rendered incompetent to give evidence in any court of law or equity in consequence of his opinions on the subject of religion.

Section 20. Military Subordinate to Civil Power

The military shall be in strict subordination to the civil power.

Section 21. Rights of Suitors

(1) Writs of error shall never be prohibited, and shall be issued by such courts as the legislature designates by law.

(2) In any court of this state, any suitor may prosecute or defend his suit either in his own proper person or by an attorney of the suitor's choice.

Section 22. Maintenance of Free Government

The blessings of a free government can only be maintained by a firm adherence to justice, moderation, temperance, frugality and virtue, and by frequent recurrence to fundamental principles.

Section 23. Transportation of School Children

Nothing in this constitution shall prohibit the legislature from providing for the safety and welfare of children by providing for the transportation of children to and from any parochial or private school or institution of learning.

Section 24. Use of School Buildings

Nothing in this constitution shall prohibit the legislature from authorizing, by law, the use of public school buildings by civic, religious or charitable organizations during non-school hours upon payment by the organization to the school district of reasonable compensation for such use.

Section 25. Right to Keep and Bear Arms

The people have the right to keep and bear arms for security, defense, hunting, recreation or any other lawful purpose.

Section 26. Right to Fish, Hunt, Trap, and Take Game

The people have the right to fish, hunt, trap, and take game subject only to reasonable restrictions as prescribed by law.

ARTICLE II: BOUNDARIES

Section 1. State Boundary

It is hereby ordained and declared that the state of Wisconsin doth consent and accept of the boundaries prescribed in the act of congress entitled "An act to enable the people of Wisconsin territory to form a constitution and state government, and for the admission of such state into the Union," approved August sixth, one thousand eight hundred and forty–six, to wit: Beginning at the northeast corner of the state of Illinois—that is to say, at a point in the center of Lake Michigan where the line of forty–two degrees and thirty minutes of north latitude crosses the same; thence running with the boundary line of the state of Michigan, through Lake Michigan, Green Bay, to the mouth of the Menominee river; thence up the channel of the said river to the Brule river; thence up said last– mentioned river to Lake Brule; thence along the southern shore of Lake Brule in a direct line to the center of the channel between Middle and South Islands, in the Lake of the Desert; thence in a direct line to the head waters of the Montreal river, as marked upon the survey made by Captain Cramm; thence down the main channel of the Montreal river to the middle of Lake Superior; thence through the center of Lake Superior to the mouth of the St. Louis river; thence up the main channel of said river to the first rapids in the same, above the Indian village, according to Nicollet's map; thence due south to the main branch of the river St. Croix; thence down the main channel of said river to the Mississippi; thence down the center of the main channel of that river to the northwest corner of the state of Illinois; thence due east with the northern boundary of the state of Illinois to the place of beginning, as established by "An act to enable the people of the Illinois territory to form a constitution and state government, and for the admission of such state into the Union on an equal footing with the original states," approved April 18th, 1818.

Section 2. Enabling Act Accepted

The propositions contained in the act of congress are hereby accepted, ratified and confirmed, and shall remain irrevocable without the consent of the United States; and it is hereby ordained that this state shall never interfere with the primary disposal of the soil within the same by the United States, nor with any regulations congress may find necessary for securing the title in such soil to bona fide purchasers thereof; and in no case shall nonresident proprietors be taxed higher than residents. Provided, that nothing in this constitution, or in the act of congress aforesaid, shall in any manner prejudice or affect the right of the state of Wisconsin to 500,000 acres of land granted to said state, and to be hereafter selected and located by and under the act of congress entitled "An act to appropriate the proceeds of the sales of the public lands, and grant preemption rights," approved September fourth, one thousand eight hundred and forty-one.

ARTICLE III: SUFFRAGE

Section 1. Electors

Every United States citizen age 18 or older who is a resident of an election district in this state is a qualified elector of that district.

Section 2. Implementation

Laws may be enacted:

(1) Defining residency.

(2) Providing for registration of electors.

(3) Providing for absentee voting.

(4) Excluding from the right of suffrage persons:

(a) Convicted of a felony, unless restored to civil rights.

(b) Adjudged by a court to be incompetent or partially incompetent, unless the judgment specifies that the person is capable of understanding the objective of the elective process or the judgment is set aside.

(5) Subject to ratification by the people at a general election, extending the right of suffrage to additional classes.

Section 3. Secret Ballot

All votes shall be by secret ballot.

Section 4. Residence Saved

Repealed

Section 5. Military Stationing Does Not Confer Residence

Repealed

Section 6. Exclusion from Suffrage

Repealed

ARTICLE IV: LEGISLATIVE

Section 1. Legislative Power

The legislative power shall be vested in a senate and assembly.

Section 2. Legislature, How Constituted

The number of the members of the assembly shall never be less than fifty-four nor more than one hundred. The senate shall consist of a number not more than one-third nor less than one-fourth of the number of the members of the assembly.

Section 3. Apportionment

At its first session after each enumeration made by the authority of the United States, the legislature shall apportion and district anew the members of the senate and assembly, according to the number of inhabitants.

Section 4. Representatives to the Assembly, How Chosen

The members of the assembly shall be chosen biennially, by single districts, on the Tuesday succeeding the first Monday of November in even- numbered years, by the qualified electors of the several districts, such districts to be bounded by county, precinct, town or ward lines, to consist of contiguous territory and be in as compact form as practicable.

Section 5. Senators, How Chosen

The senators shall be elected by single districts of convenient contiguous territory, at the same time and in the same manner as members of the assembly are required to be chosen; and no assembly district shall be divided in the formation of a senate district. The senate districts shall be numbered in the regular series, and the senators shall be chosen alternately from the odd and even-numbered districts for the term of 4 years.

Section 6. Qualifications of Legislators

No person shall be eligible to the legislature who shall not have resided one year within the state, and be a qualified elector in the district which he may be chosen to represent.

Section 7. Organization of Legislature; Quorum; Compulsory Attendance

Each house shall be the judge of the elections, returns and qualifications of its own members; and a majority of each shall constitute a quorum to do business, but a smaller number may adjourn from day to day, and may compel the attendance of absent members in such manner and under such penalties as each house may provide.

Section 8. Rules; Contempts; Expulsion

Each house may determine the rules of its own proceedings, punish for contempt and disorderly behavior, and with the concurrence of two− thirds of all the members elected, expel a member; but no member shall be expelled a second time for the same cause.

Section 9. Officers

Each house shall choose its presiding officers from its own members.

Section 9 (2). The legislature shall provide by law for the establishment of a department of transportation and a transportation fund.

Section 10. Journals; Open Doors; Adjournments

Each house shall keep a journal of its proceedings and publish the same, except such parts as require secrecy. The doors of each house shall be kept open except when the public welfare shall require secrecy. Neither house shall, without consent of the other, adjourn for more than three days.

Section 11. Meeting of Legislature

The legislature shall meet at the seat of government at such time as shall be provided by law, unless convened by the governor in special session, and when so convened no business shall be transacted except as shall be necessary to accomplish the special purposes for which it was convened.

Section 12. Ineligibility of Legislators to Office

No member of the legislature shall, during the term for which he was elected, be appointed or elected to any civil office in the state, which shall have been created, or the emoluments of which shall have been increased, during the term for which he was elected.

Section 13. Ineligibility of Federal Officers

No person being a member of congress, or holding any military or civil office under the United States, shall be eligible to a seat in the legislature; and if any person shall, after his election as a member of the legislature, be elected to congress, or be appointed to any office, civil or military, under the government of the United States, his acceptance thereof shall vacate his seat. This restriction shall not prohibit a legislator from accepting short periods of active duty as a member of the reserve or from serving in the armed forces during any emergency declared by the executive.

Section 14. Filling Vacancies

The governor shall issue writs of election to fill such vacancies as may occur in either house of the legislature.

Section 15. Exemption from Arrest and Civil Process

Members of the legislature shall in all cases, except treason, felony and breach of the peace, be privileged from arrest; nor shall they be subject to any civil process, during the session of the legislature, nor for fifteen days next before the commencement and after the termination of each session.

Section 16. Privilege in Debate

No member of the legislature shall be liable in any civil action, or criminal prosecution whatever, for words spoken in debate.

Section 17. Enactment of Laws

(1) The style of all laws of the state shall be "The people of the state of Wisconsin, represented in senate and assembly, do enact as follows:".

(2) No law shall be enacted except by bill. No law shall be in force until published.

(3) The legislature shall provide by law for the speedy publication of all laws.

Section 18. Title of Private Bills

No private or local bill which may be passed by the legislature shall embrace more than one subject, and that shall be expressed in the title.

Section 19. Origin of Bills

Any bill may originate in either house of the legislature, and a bill passed by one house may be amended by the other.

Section 20. Yeas and Nays

The yeas and nays of the members of either house on any question shall, at the request of one-sixth of those present, be entered on the journal.

Section 21. Compensation of Members

Repealed

Section 22. Powers of County Boards

The legislature may confer upon the boards of supervisors of the several counties of the state such powers of a local, legislative and administrative character as they shall from time to time prescribe.

Section 23. Town and County Government

The legislature shall establish but one system of town government, which shall be as nearly uniform as practicable; but the legislature may provide for the election at large once in every 4 years of a chief executive officer in any county with such powers of an administrative character as they may from time to time prescribe in accordance with this section and shall establish one or more systems of county government.

Section 23a. Chief Executive Officer to Approve or Veto

Resolutions or Ordinances; Proceedings on Veto
Every resolution or ordinance passed by the county board in any county shall, before it becomes effective, be presented to the chief executive officer. If he approves, he shall sign it; if not, he shall return it with his objections, which objections shall be entered at large upon the journal and the board shall proceed to reconsider the matter. Appropriations may be approved in whole or in part by the chief executive officer and the part approved shall become law, and the part objected to shall be returned in

the same manner as provided for in other resolutions or ordinances. If, after such reconsideration, two-thirds of the members-elect of the county board agree to pass the resolution or ordinance or the part of the resolution or ordinance objected to, it shall become effective on the date prescribed but not earlier than the date of passage following reconsideration. In all such cases, the votes of the members of the county board shall be determined by ayes and noes and the names of the members voting for or against the resolution or ordinance or the part thereof objected to shall be entered on the journal. If any resolution or ordinance is not returned by the chief executive officer to the county board at its first meeting occurring not less than 6 days, Sundays excepted, after it has been presented to him, it shall become effective unless the county board has recessed or adjourned for a period in excess of 60 days, in which case it shall not be effective without his approval.

Section 24. Gambling

(1) Except as provided in this section, the legislature may not authorize gambling in any form.

(2) Except as otherwise provided by law, the following activities do not constitute consideration as an element of gambling:

(a) To listen to or watch a television or radio program.

(b) To fill out a coupon or entry blank, whether or not proof of purchase is required.

(c) To visit a mercantile establishment or other place without being required to make a purchase or pay an admittance fee.

(3) The legislature may authorize the following bingo games licensed by the state, but all profits shall accrue to the licensed organization and no salaries, fees or profits may be paid to any other organization or person: bingo games operated by religious, charitable, service, fraternal or veterans' organizations or those to which contributions are deductible for federal or state income tax purposes. All moneys received by the state that are attributable to bingo games shall be used for property tax relief for residents of this state as provided by law. The distribution of moneys that are attributable to bingo games may not vary based on the income or age of the person provided the property tax relief. The distribution of moneys that are attributable to bingo games shall not be subject to the uniformity requirement of section 1 of article VIII. In this subsection, the distribution of all moneys attributable to bingo games shall include any earnings on the moneys received by the state that are attributable to bingo games, but shall not include any moneys used for the regulation of, and enforcement of law relating to, bingo games.

(4) The legislature may authorize the following raffle games licensed by the state, but all profits shall accrue to the licensed local organization and no salaries, fees or profits may be paid to any other organization or person: raffle games operated by local religious, charitable, service, fraternal or veterans' organizations or those to which contributions are deductible for federal or state income tax purposes. The legislature shall limit the number of raffles conducted by any such organization.

(5) This section shall not prohibit pari−mutuel on−track betting as provided by law. The state may not own or operate any facility or enterprise for pari−mutuel betting, or lease any state−owned land to any other owner or operator for such purposes. All moneys received by the state that are attributable to pari−mutuel on−track betting shall be used for property tax relief for residents of this state as provided by law. The distribution of moneys that are attributable to pari−mutuel on−track betting may not vary based on the income or age of the person provided the property tax relief. The distribution of moneys that are attributable to pari−mutuel on−track betting shall not be subject to the uniformity requirement of section 1 of article VIII. In this subsection, the distribution of all moneys attributable to pari−mutuel on−track betting shall include any earnings on the moneys received by the state that are attributable to pari-mutuel on- track betting, but shall not include any moneys used for the regulation of, and enforcement of law relating to, pari-mutuel on-track betting.

(6) (a) The legislature may authorize the creation of a lottery to be operated by the state as provided by law. The expenditure of public funds or of revenues derived from lottery operations to engage in promotional advertising of the Wisconsin state lottery is prohibited. Any advertising of the state lottery shall indicate the odds of a specific lottery ticket to be selected as the winning ticket for each prize amount offered. The net proceeds of the state lottery shall be deposited in the treasury of the state, to be used for property tax relief for residents of this state as provided by law. The distribution of the net proceeds of the state lottery may not vary based on the income or age of the person provided the property tax relief. The distribution of the net proceeds of the state lottery shall not be subject to the uniformity requirement of section 1 of article VIII. In this paragraph, the distribution of the net proceeds of the state lottery shall include any earnings on the net proceeds of the state lottery.

(b) The lottery authorized under par. (a) shall be an enterprise that entitles the player, by purchasing a ticket, to participate in a game of chance if: 1) the winning tickets are randomly predetermined and the player reveals preprinted numbers or symbols from which it can be immediately determined whether the ticket is a winning ticket entitling the player to win a prize as prescribed in the features and procedures for the game, including an opportunity to win a prize in a secondary or subsequent chance drawing or game; or 2) the ticket is evidence of the numbers or symbols selected by the player or, at the player's option, selected by a computer, and the player becomes entitled to a prize as prescribed in the features and procedures for the game, including an opportunity to win a prize in a secondary or subsequent chance drawing or game if some or all of the player's symbols or numbers are selected in a chance drawing or game, if the player's ticket is randomly selected by the computer at the time of purchase or if the ticket is selected in a chance drawing.

(c) Notwithstanding the authorization of a state lottery under par. (a), the following games, or games simulating any of the following games, may not be conducted by the state as a lottery:

(1) any game in which winners are selected based on the results of a race or sporting event;

(2) any banking card game, including blackjack, baccarat or chemin de fer;

(3) poker;

(4) roulette;

(5) craps or any other game that involves rolling dice;

(6) keno;

(7) bingo 21, bingo jack, bingolet or bingo craps;

(8) any game of chance that is placed on a slot machine or any mechanical, electromechanical or electronic device that is generally available to be played at a gambling casino;

(9) any game or device that is commonly known as a video game of chance or a video gaming machine or that is commonly considered to be a video gambling machine, unless such machine is a video device operated by the state in a game authorized under par. (a) to permit the sale of tickets through retail outlets under contract with the state and the device does not determine or indicate whether the player has won a prize, other than by verifying that the player's ticket or some or all of the player's symbols or numbers on the player's ticket have been selected in a chance drawing, or by verifying that the player's ticket has been randomly selected by a central system computer at the time of purchase;

(10) any game that is similar to a game listed in this paragraph;

or

(11) any other game that is commonly considered to be a form of gambling and is not, or is not substantially similar to, a game conducted by the state under par.(a). No game conducted by the state under par.(a) may permit a player of the game to purchase a ticket, or to otherwise participate in the game, from a residence by using a computer, telephone or other form of electronic, telecommunication, video or technological aid.

Section 25. Stationery and Printing

The legislature shall provide by law that all stationery required for the use of the state, and all printing authorized and required by them to be done for their use, or for the state, shall be let by contract to the lowest bidder, but the legislature may establish a maximum price; no member of the legislature or other state officer shall be interested, either directly or indirectly, in any such contract.

Section 26. Extra Compensation; Salary Change

(1) The legislature may not grant any extra compensation to a public officer, agent, servant or contractor after the services have been rendered or the contract has been entered into.

(2) Except as provided in this subsection, the compensation of a public officer may not be increased or diminished during the term of office:

(a) When any increase or decrease in the compensation of justices of the supreme court or judges of any court of record becomes effective as to any such justice or judge, it shall be effective from such date as to every such justice or judge.

(b) Any increase in the compensation of members of the legislature shall take effect, for all senators and representatives to the assembly, after the next general election beginning with the new assembly term.

(3) Subsection (1) shall not apply to increased benefits for persons who have been or shall be granted benefits of any kind under a retirement system when such increased benefits are provided by a legislative act passed on a call of ayes and noes by a three-fourths vote of all the members elected to both houses of the legislature and such act provides for sufficient state funds to cover the costs of the increased benefits.

Section 27. Suits Against State

The legislature shall direct by law in what manner and in what courts suits may be brought against the state.

Section 28. Oath of Office

Members of the legislature, and all officers, executive and judicial, except such inferior officers as may be by law exempted, shall before they enter upon the duties of their respective offices, take and subscribe an oath or affirmation to support the constitution of the United States and the constitution of the state of Wisconsin, and faithfully to discharge the duties of their respective offices to the best of their ability.

Section 29. Militia

The legislature shall determine what persons shall constitute the militia of the state, and may provide for organizing and disciplining the same in such manner as shall be prescribed by law.

Section 30. Elections by Legislature

All elections made by the legislature shall be by roll call vote entered in the journals.

Section 31. Special and Private Laws Prohibited

The legislature is prohibited from enacting any special or private laws in the following cases:

(1) For changing the names of persons, constituting one person the heir at law of another or granting any divorce.

(2) For laying out, opening or altering highways, except in cases of state roads extending into more than one county, and military roads to aid in the construction of which lands may be granted by congress.

(3) For authorizing persons to keep ferries across streams at points wholly within this state.

(4) For authorizing the sale or mortgage of real or personal property of minors or others under disability.

(5) For locating or changing any county seat.

(6) For assessment or collection of taxes or for extending the time for the collection thereof.

(7) For granting corporate powers or privileges, except to cities.

(8) For authorizing the apportionment of any part of the school fund.

(9) For incorporating any city, town or village, or to amend the charter thereof.

Section 32. General Laws on Enumerated Subjects

The legislature may provide by general law for the treatment of any subject for which lawmaking is prohibited by section 31 of this article. Subject to reasonable classifications, such laws shall be uniform in their operation throughout the state.

Section 33. Auditing of State Accounts

The legislature shall provide for the auditing of state accounts and may establish such offices and prescribe such duties for the same as it shall deem necessary.

Section 34. Continuity of Civil Government

The legislature, in order to ensure continuity of state and local governmental operations in periods of emergency resulting from enemy action in the form of an attack, shall

(1) forthwith provide for prompt and temporary succession to the powers and duties of public offices, of whatever nature and whether filled by election or appointment, the incumbents of which may become unavailable for carrying on the powers and duties of such offices, and

(2) adopt such other measures as may be necessary and proper for attaining the objectives of this section.

ARTICLE V: EXECUTIVE

Section 1. Governor; Lieutenant Governor; Term

The executive power shall be vested in a governor who shall hold office for 4 years; a lieutenant governor shall be elected at the same time and for the same term.

Section 1m. Governor; 4–year Term

Repealed

Section 1n. Lieutenant Governor; 4–year Term

Repealed

Section 2. Eligibility

No person except a citizen of the United States and a qualified elector of the state shall be eligible to the office of governor or lieutenant governor.

Section 3. Election

The governor and lieutenant governor shall be elected by the qualified electors of the state at the times and places of choosing members of the legislature. They shall be chosen jointly, by the casting by each voter of a single vote applicable to both offices beginning with the general election in 1970. The persons respectively having the highest number of votes cast jointly for them for governor and lieutenant governor shall be elected; but in case two or more slates shall have an equal and the highest number of votes for governor and lieutenant governor, the two houses of the legislature, at its next annual session shall forthwith, by joint ballot, choose one of the slates so having an equal and the highest number of votes for governor and lieutenant governor. The returns of election for governor and lieutenant governor shall be made in such manner as shall be provided by law.

Section 4. Powers and Duties

The governor shall be commander in chief of the military and naval forces of the state. He shall have power to convene the legislature on extraordinary occasions, and in case of invasion, or danger from the prevalence of contagious disease at the seat of government, he may convene them at any other suitable place within the state. He shall communicate to the legislature, at every session, the condition of the state, and recommend such matters to them for their consideration as he may deem expedient. He shall transact all necessary business with the officers of the government, civil and military. He shall expedite all such measures as may be resolved upon by the legislature, and shall take care that the laws be faithfully executed.

Section 5. Compensation of Governor

Repealed

Section 6. Pardoning Power

The governor shall have power to grant reprieves, commutations and pardons, after conviction, for all offenses, except treason and cases of impeachment, upon such conditions and with such restrictions and limitations as he may think proper, subject to such regulations as may be provided by law relative to the manner of applying for pardons. Upon conviction for treason he shall have the power to suspend the execution of the sentence until the case shall be reported to the legislature at its next meeting, when the legislature shall either pardon, or commute the sentence, direct the execution of the sentence, or grant a further reprieve. He shall annually communicate to the legislature each case of reprieve, commutation or pardon granted, stating the name of the convict, the crime of which he was convicted, the sentence and its date, and the date of the commutation, pardon or reprieve, with his reasons for granting the same.

Section 7. Lieutenant Governor, When Governor

(1) Upon the governor's death, resignation or removal from office, the lieutenant governor shall become governor for the balance of the unexpired term.

(2) If the governor is absent from this state, impeached, or from mental or physical disease, becomes incapable of performing the duties of the office, the lieutenant governor shall serve as acting governor for the balance of the unexpired term or until the governor returns, the disability ceases or the impeachment is vacated. But when the governor, with the consent of the legislature, shall be out of this state in time of war at the head of the state's military force, the governor shall continue as commander in chief of the military force.

Section 8. Secretary of State, When Governor

(1) If there is a vacancy in the office of lieutenant governor and the governor dies, resigns or is removed from office, the secretary of state shall become governor for the balance of the unexpired term.

(2) If there is a vacancy in the office of lieutenant governor and the governor is absent from this state, impeached, or from mental or physical disease becomes incapable of performing the duties of the office, the secretary of state shall serve as acting governor for the balance of the unexpired term or until the governor returns, the disability ceases or the impeachment is vacated.

Section 9. Compensation of Lieutenant Governor

Section 10. Governor to Approve or Veto Bills; Proceedings on Veto

(1) (a) Every bill which shall have passed the legislature shall, before it becomes a law, be presented to the governor.

(b) If the governor approves and signs the bill, the bill shall become law. Appropriation bills may be approved in whole or in part by the governor, and the part approved shall become law.

(c) In approving an appropriation bill in part, the governor may not create a new word by rejecting individual letters in the words of the enrolled bill.

(2) (a) If the governor rejects the bill, the governor shall return the bill, together with the objections in writing, to the house in which the bill originated. The house of origin shall enter the objections at large upon the journal and proceed to reconsider the bill. If, after such reconsideration, two−thirds of the members present agree to pass the bill notwithstanding the objections of the governor, it shall be sent, together with the objections, to the other house, by which it shall likewise be reconsidered, and if approved by two−thirds of the members present it shall become law.

(b) The rejected part of an appropriation bill, together with the governor's objections in writing, shall be returned to the house in which the bill originated. The house of origin shall enter the objections at large upon the journal and proceed to reconsider the rejected part of the appropriation bill. If, after such reconsideration, two−thirds of the members present agree to approve the rejected part notwithstanding the objections of the governor, it shall be sent, together with the objections, to the other house, by which it shall likewise be reconsidered, and if approved by two−thirds of the members present the rejected part shall become law.

(c) In all such cases the votes of both houses shall be determined by ayes and noes, and the names of the members voting for or against passage of the bill or the rejected part of the bill notwithstanding the objections of the governor shall be entered on the journal of each house respectively.

(3) Any bill not returned by the governor within 6 days (Sundays excepted) after it shall have been presented to the governor shall be law unless the legislature, by final adjournment, prevents the bill's return, in which case it shall not be law.

ARTICLE VI: ADMINISTRATIVE

Section 1. Election of Secretary of State, Treasurer and Attorney General; Term

The qualified electors of this state, at the times and places of choosing the members of the legislature, shall in 1970 and every 4 years thereafter elect a secretary of state, treasurer and attorney general who shall hold their offices for 4 years.

Section 1m. Secretary of State; 4-year Term

Repealed

Section 1n. Treasurer; 4-year Term

Repealed

Section 1p. Attorney General; 4-year Term

Repealed

Section 2. Secretary of State; Duties, Compensation

The secretary of state shall keep a fair record of the official acts of the legislature and executive department of the state, and shall, when required, lay the same and all matters relative thereto before either branch of the legislature. He shall perform such other duties as shall be assigned him by law. He shall receive as a compensation for his services yearly such sum as shall be provided by law, and shall keep his office at the seat of government.

Section 3. Treasurer and Attorney General; Duties, Compensation

The powers, duties and compensation of the treasurer and attorney general shall be prescribed by law.

Section 4. County Officers; Election, Terms, Removal; Vacancies

(1) (a) Except as provided in pars. (b) and (c) and sub. (2), coroners, registers of deeds, district attorneys, and all other elected county officers, except judicial officers, sheriffs, and chief executive officers, shall be chosen by the electors of the respective counties once in every 2 years.

(b) Beginning with the first general election at which the governor is elected which occurs after the ratification of this paragraph, sheriffs shall be chosen by the electors of the respective counties, or by the electors of all of the respective counties comprising each combination of counties combined by the legislature for that purpose, for the term of 4 years and coroners in counties in which there is a coroner shall be chosen by the electors of the respective counties, or by the electors of all of the respective counties comprising each combination of counties combined by the legislature for that purpose, for the term of 4 years.

(c) Beginning with the first general election at which the president is elected which occurs after the ratification of this paragraph, district attorneys, registers of deeds, county clerks, and treasurers shall be chosen by the electors of the respective counties, or by the electors of all of the respective counties comprising each combination of counties combined by the legislature for that purpose, for the term of 4 years and surveyors in counties in which the office of surveyor is filled by election shall be chosen by the electors of the respective counties, or by the electors of all of the respective counties comprising each combination of counties combined by the legislature for that purpose, for the term of 4 years.

(2) The offices of coroner and surveyor in counties having a population of 500,000 or more are abolished. Counties not having a population of 500,000 shall have the option of retaining the elective office of coroner or instituting a medical examiner system. Two or more counties may institute a joint medical examiner system.

(3) (a) Sheriffs may not hold any other partisan office.

(b) Sheriffs may be required by law to renew their security from time to time, and in default of giving such new security their office shall be deemed vacant.

(4) The governor may remove any elected county officer mentioned in this section except a county clerk, treasurer, or surveyor, giving to the officer a copy of the charges and an opportunity of being heard.

(5) All vacancies in the offices of coroner, register of deeds or district attorney shall be filled by appointment. The person appointed to fill a vacancy shall hold office only for the unexpired portion of the term to which appointed and until a successor shall be elected and qualified.

(6) When a vacancy occurs in the office of sheriff, the vacancy shall be filled by appointment of the governor, and the person appointed shall serve until his or her successor is elected and qualified.

ARTICLE VII: JUDICIARY

Section 1. Impeachment; Trial

The court for the trial of impeachments shall be composed of the senate. The assembly shall have the power of impeaching all civil officers of this state for corrupt conduct in office, or for crimes and misdemeanors; but a majority of all the members elected shall concur in an impeachment. On the trial of an impeachment against the governor, the lieutenant governor shall not act as a member of the court. No judicial officer shall exercise his office, after he shall have been impeached, until his acquittal. Before the trial of an impeachment the members of the court shall take an oath or affirmation truly and impartially to try the impeachment according to evidence; and no person shall be convicted without the concurrence of two-thirds of the members present. Judgment in cases of impeachment shall not extend further than to removal from office, or removal from office and disqualification to hold any office of honor, profit or trust under the state; but the party impeached shall be liable to indictment, trial and punishment according to law.

Section 2. Court System

The judicial power of this state shall be vested in a unified court system consisting of one supreme court, a court of appeals, a circuit court, such trial courts of general uniform statewide jurisdiction as the legislature may create by law, and a municipal court if authorized by the legislature under section 14.

Section 3. Supreme Court: Jurisdiction

(1) The supreme court shall have superintending and administrative authority over all courts.

(2) The supreme court has appellate jurisdiction over all courts and may hear original actions and proceedings. The supreme court may issue all writs necessary in aid of its jurisdiction.

(3) The supreme court may review judgments and orders of the court of appeals, may remove cases from the court of appeals and may accept cases on certification by the court of appeals.

Section 4. Supreme Court: Election, Chief Justice, Court System Administration

(1) The supreme court shall have 7 members who shall be known as justices of the supreme court. Justices shall be elected for 10-year terms of office commencing with the August 1 next succeeding the election. Only one justice may be elected in any year. Any 4 justices shall constitute a quorum for the conduct of the court's business.

(2) The chief justice of the supreme court shall be elected for a term of 2 years by a majority of the justices then serving on the court. The justice so designated as chief justice may, irrevocably, decline to serve as chief justice or resign as chief justice but continue to serve as a justice of the supreme court.

(3) The chief justice of the supreme court shall be the administrative head of the judicial system and shall exercise this administrative authority pursuant to procedures adopted by the supreme court. The chief justice may assign any judge of a court of record to aid in the proper disposition of judicial business in any court of record except the supreme court.

Section 5. Judicial Circuits

Repealed

Section 5. Court of Appeals

(1) The legislature shall by law combine the judicial circuits of the state into one or more districts for the court of appeals and shall designate in each district the locations where the appeals court shall sit for the convenience of litigants.

(2) For each district of the appeals court there shall be chosen by the qualified electors of the district one or more appeals judges as prescribed by law, who shall sit as prescribed by law. Appeals judges shall be elected for 6-year terms and shall reside in the district from which elected. No alteration of district or circuit boundaries shall have the effect of removing an appeals judge from office during the judge's term. In case of an increase in the number of appeals judges, the first judge or judges shall be elected for full terms unless the legislature prescribes a shorter initial term for staggering of terms.

(3) The appeals court shall have such appellate jurisdiction in the district, including jurisdiction to review administrative proceedings, as the legislature may provide by law, but shall have no original jurisdiction other than by prerogative writ. The appeals court may issue all writs necessary in aid of its jurisdiction and shall have supervisory authority over all actions and proceedings in the courts in the district.

Section 6. Circuit Court: Boundaries

The legislature shall prescribe by law the number of judicial circuits, making them as compact and convenient as practicable, and bounding them by county lines. No alteration of circuit boundaries shall have the effect of removing a circuit judge from office during the judge's term. In case of an increase of circuits, the first judge or judges shall be elected.

Section 7. Circuit Court: Election

For each circuit there shall be chosen by the qualified electors thereof one or more circuit judges as prescribed by law. Circuit judges shall be elected for 6-year terms and shall reside in the circuit from which elected.

Section 8. Circuit Court: Jurisdiction

Except as otherwise provided by law, the circuit court shall have original jurisdiction in all matters civil and criminal within this state and such appellate jurisdiction in the circuit as the legislature may prescribe by law. The circuit court may issue all writs necessary in aid of its jurisdiction.

Section 9. Judicial Elections, Vacancies

When a vacancy occurs in the office of justice of the supreme court or judge of any court of record, the vacancy shall be filled by appointment by the governor, which shall continue until a successor is elected and qualified. There shall be no election for a justice or judge at the partisan general election for state or county officers, nor within 30 days either before or after such election.

Section 10. Judges: Eligibility to Office

(1) No justice of the supreme court or judge of any court of record shall hold any other office of public trust, except a judicial office, during the term for which elected. No person shall be eligible to the office of judge who shall not, at the time of election or appointment, be a qualified elector within the jurisdiction for which chosen.

(2) Justices of the supreme court and judges of the courts of record shall receive such compensation as the legislature may authorize by law, but may not receive fees of office.

Section 11. Terms of Courts; Change of Judges

Repealed

Section 11. Disciplinary Proceedings

Each justice or judge shall be subject to reprimand, censure, suspension, removal for cause or for disability, by the supreme court pursuant to procedures established by the legislature by law. No justice or judge removed for cause shall be eligible for reappointment or temporary service. This section is alternative to, and cumulative with, the methods of removal provided in sections 1 and 13 of this article and section 12 of article XIII.

Section 12. Clerks of Circuit and Supreme Courts

(1) There shall be a clerk of circuit court chosen in each county organized for judicial purposes by the qualified electors thereof, who, except as provided in sub. (2), shall hold office for two years, subject to removal as provided by law.

(2) Beginning with the first general election at which the governor is elected which occurs after the ratification of this subsection, a clerk of circuit court shall be chosen by the electors of each county, for the term of 4 years, subject to removal as provided by law.

(3) In case of a vacancy, the judge of the circuit court may appoint a clerk until the vacancy is filled by an election.

(4) The clerk of circuit court shall give such security as the legislature requires by law.

(5) The supreme court shall appoint its own clerk, and may appoint a clerk of circuit court to be the clerk of the supreme court.

Section 13. Justices and Judges: Removal by Address

Any justice or judge may be removed from office by address of both houses of the legislature, if two-thirds of all the members elected to each house concur therein, but no removal shall be made by virtue of this section unless the justice or judge complained of is served with a copy of the charges, as the ground of address, and has had an opportunity of being heard. On the question of removal, the ayes and noes shall be entered on the journals.

Section 14. Municipal Court

The legislature by law may authorize each city, village and town to establish a municipal court. All municipal courts shall have uniform jurisdiction limited to actions and proceedings arising under ordinances of the municipality in which established. Judges of municipal courts may receive such compensation as provided by the municipality in which established, but may not receive fees of office.

Section 15. Justices of the Peace

Repealed

Section 16. Tribunals of Conciliation

Repealed

Section 17. Style of Writs; Indictments

Repealed

Section 18. Suit Tax

Repealed

Section 19. Testimony in Equity Suits; Master in Chancery

Repealed

Section 20. Rights of Suitors

Repealed

Section 21. Publication of Laws and Decisions

Repealed

Section 22. Commissioners to Revise Code of Practice

Repealed

Section 23. Court Commissioners

Repealed

Section 24. Justices and Judges: Eligibility for Office; Retirement

(1) To be eligible for the office of supreme court justice or judge of any court of record, a person must be an attorney licensed to practice law in this state and have been so licensed for 5 years immediately prior to election or appointment.

(2) Unless assigned temporary service under subsection (3), no person may serve as a supreme court justice or judge of a court of record beyond the July 31 following the date on which such person attains that age, of not less than 70 years, which the legislature shall prescribe by law.

(3) A person who has served as a supreme court justice or judge of a court of record may, as provided by law, serve as a judge of any court of record except the supreme court on a temporary basis if assigned by the chief justice of the supreme court.

ARTICLE VIII: FINANCE

Section 1. Rule of Taxation Uniform; Income, Privilege and Occupation Taxes

The rule of taxation shall be uniform but the legislature may empower cities, villages or towns to collect and return taxes on real estate located therein by optional methods. Taxes shall be levied upon such property with such classifications as to forests and minerals including or separate or severed from the land, as the legislature shall prescribe. Taxation of agricultural land and undeveloped land, both as defined by law, need not be uniform with the taxation of each other nor with the taxation of other real property. Taxation of merchants' stock–in–trade, manufacturers' materials and finished products, and livestock need not be uniform with the taxation of real property and other personal property, but the taxation of all such merchants' stock–in–trade, manufacturers' materials and finished products and livestock shall be uniform, except that the legislature may provide that the value thereof shall be determined on an average basis. Taxes may also be imposed on incomes, privileges and occupations, which taxes may be graduated and progressive, and reasonable exemptions may be provided.

Section 2. Appropriations; Limitation

No money shall be paid out of the treasury except in pursuance of an appropriation by law. No appropriation shall be made for the payment of any claim against the state except claims of the United States and judgments, unless filed within six years after the claim accrued.

Section 3. Credit of State

Except as provided in s. 7 (2) (a), the credit of the state shall never be given, or loaned, in aid of any individual, association or corporation.

Section 4. Contracting State Debts

The state shall never contract any public debt except in the cases and manner herein provided.

Section 5. Annual Tax Levy to Equal Expenses

The legislature shall provide for an annual tax sufficient to defray the estimated expenses of the state for each year; and whenever the expenses of any year shall exceed the income, the legislature shall provide for levying a tax for the ensuing year, sufficient, with other sources of income, to pay the deficiency as well as the estimated expenses of such ensuing year.

Section 6. Public Debt for Extraordinary Expense; Taxation

For the purpose of defraying extraordinary expenditures the state may contract public debts (but such debts shall never in the aggregate exceed one hundred thousand dollars). Every such debt shall be authorized by law, for some purpose or purposes to be distinctly specified therein; and the vote of a majority of all the members elected to each house, to be taken by yeas and nays, shall be necessary to the passage of such law; and every such law shall provide for levying an annual tax sufficient to pay the annual interest of such debt and the principal within five years from the passage of such law, and shall specially appropriate the proceeds of such taxes to the payment of such principal and interest; and such appropriation shall not be repealed, nor the taxes be postponed or diminished, until the principal and interest of such debt shall have been wholly paid.

Section 7. Public Debt for Public Defense; Bonding for Public Purposes

(1) The legislature may also borrow money to repel invasion, suppress insurrection, or defend the state in time of war; but the money thus raised shall be applied exclusively to the object for which the loan was authorized, or to the repayment of the debt thereby created.

(2) Any other provision of this constitution to the contrary notwithstanding:

(a) The state may contract public debt and pledges to the payment thereof its full faith, credit and taxing power:

1. To acquire, construct, develop, extend, enlarge or improve land, waters, property, highways, railways, buildings, equipment or facilities for public purposes.

2. To make funds available for veterans' housing loans.

(b) The aggregate public debt contracted by the state in any calendar year pursuant to paragraph (a) shall not exceed an amount equal to the lesser of:

1. Three-fourths of one per centum of the aggregate value of all taxable property in the state; or

2. Five per centum of the aggregate value of all taxable property in the state less the sum of: a. the aggregate public debt of the state contracted pursuant to this section outstanding as of January 1 of such calendar year after subtracting therefrom the amount of sinking funds on hand on January 1 of such calendar year which are applicable exclusively to repayment of such outstanding
public debt and, b. the outstanding indebtedness as of January 1 of such calendar year of any entity of the type described in paragraph (d) to the extent that such indebtedness is supported by or payable from payments out of the treasury of the state.

(c) The state may contract public debt, without limit, to fund or refund the whole or any part of any public debt contracted pursuant to paragraph (a), including any premium payable with respect thereto and any interest to accrue thereon, or to fund or refund the whole or any part of any indebtedness incurred prior to January 1, 1972, by any entity of the type described in paragraph (d), including any premium payable with respect thereto and any interest to accrue thereon.

(d) No money shall be paid out of the treasury, with respect to any lease, sublease or other agreement entered into after January 1, 1971, to the Wisconsin State Agencies Building Corporation, Wisconsin State Colleges Building Corporation, Wisconsin State Public Building Corporation, Wisconsin University Building Corporation or any similar entity existing or operating for similar purposes pursuant to which such nonprofit corporation or such other entity undertakes to finance or provide a facility for use or occupancy by the state or an agency, department or instrumentality thereof.

(e) The legislature shall prescribe all matters relating to the contracting of public debt pursuant to paragraph (a), including: the public purposes for which public debt may be contracted; by vote of a majority of the members elected to each of the 2 houses of the legislature, the amount of public debt which may be contracted for any class of such purposes; the public debt or other indebtedness which may be funded or refunded; the kinds of notes, bonds or other evidence of public debt which may be issued by the state; and the manner in which the aggregate value of all taxable property in the state shall be determined.

(f) The full faith, credit and taxing power of the state are pledged to the payment of all public debt created on behalf of the state pursuant to this section and the legislature shall provide by appropriation for the payment of the interest upon and installments of principal of all such public debt as the same falls due, but, in any event, suit may be brought against the state to compel such payment.

(g) At any time after January 1, 1972, by vote of a majority of the members elected to each of the 2 houses of the legislature, the legislature may declare that an emergency exists and submit to the people a proposal to authorize the state to contract a specific amount of public debt for a purpose specified in such proposal, without regard to the limit provided in paragraph (b). Any such authorization shall be effective if approved by a majority of the electors voting thereon. Public debt contracted pursuant to such authorization shall thereafter be deemed to have been contracted pursuant to paragraph (a), but neither such public debt nor any public debt contracted to fund or refund such public debt shall be considered in computing the debt limit provided in paragraph (b). Not more than one such authorization shall be thus made in any 2-year period.

Section 8. Vote on Fiscal Bills; Quorum

On the passage in either house of the legislature of any law which imposes, continues or renews a tax, or creates a debt or charge, or makes, continues or renews an appropriation of public or trust money, or releases, discharges or commutes a claim or demand of the state, the question shall be taken by yeas and nays, which shall be duly entered on the journal; and three-fifths of all the members elected to such house shall in all such cases be required to constitute a quorum therein.

Section 9. Evidences of Public Debt

No scrip, certificate, or other evidence of state debt, whatsoever, shall be issued, except for such debts as are authorized by the sixth and seventh sections of this article.

Section 10. Internal Improvements

Except as further provided in this section, the state may never contract any debt for works of internal improvement, or be a party in carrying on such works.

(1) Whenever grants of land or other property shall have been made to the state, especially dedicated by the grant to particular works of internal improvement, the state may carry on such particular works and shall devote thereto the avails of such grants, and may pledge or appropriate the revenues derived from such works in aid of their completion.

(2) The state may appropriate money in the treasury or to be thereafter raised by taxation for:

(a) The construction or improvement of public highways.

(b) The development, improvement and construction of airports or other aeronautical projects.

(c) The acquisition, improvement or construction of veterans' housing.

(d) The improvement of port facilities.

(e) The acquisition, development, improvement or construction of railways and other railroad facilities.

(3) The state may appropriate moneys for the purpose of acquiring, preserving and developing the forests of the state. Of the moneys appropriated under the authority of this subsection in any one year an amount not to exceed two–tenths of one mill of the taxable property of the state as determined by the last preceding state assessment may be raised by a tax on property.

Section 11. Funds

All funds collected by the state from any taxes or fees levied or imposed for the licensing of motor vehicle operators, for the titling, licensing, or registration of motor vehicles, for motor vehicle fuel, or for the use of roadways, highways, or bridges, and from taxes and fees levied or imposed for aircraft, airline property, or aviation fuel or for railroads or railroad property shall be deposited only into the transportation fund or with a trustee for the benefit of the department of transportation or the holders of transportation-related revenue bonds, except for collections from taxes or fees in existence on December 31, 2010, that were not being deposited in the transportation fund on that date. None of the funds collected or received by the state from any source and deposited into the transportation fund shall be lapsed, further transferred, or appropriated to any program that is not directly administered by the department of transportation in furtherance of the department's responsibility for the planning, promotion, and protection of all transportation systems in the state except for programs for which there was an appropriation from the transportation fund on December 31, 2010. In this section, the term "motor vehicle" does not include any all-terrain vehicles, snowmobiles, or watercraft.

ARTICLE IX: EMINENT DOMAIN AND PROPERTY OF THE STATE

Section 1. Jurisdiction on Rivers and Lakes; Navigable Waters
The state shall have concurrent jurisdiction on all rivers and lakes bordering on this state so far as such rivers or lakes shall form a common boundary to the state and any other state or territory now or hereafter to be formed, and bounded by the same; and the river Mississippi and the navigable waters leading into the Mississippi and St. Lawrence, and the carrying places between the same, shall be common highways and forever free, as well to the inhabitants of the state as to the citizens of the United States, without any tax, impost or duty therefore.

Section 2. Territorial Property

The title to all lands and other property which have accrued to the territory of Wisconsin by grant, gift, purchase, forfeiture, escheat or otherwise shall vest in the state of Wisconsin.

Section 3. Ultimate Property in Lands; Escheats

The people of the state, in their right of sovereignty, are declared to possess the ultimate property in and to all lands within the jurisdiction of the state; and all lands the title to which shall fail from a defect of heirs shall revert or escheat to the people.

ARTICLE X: EDUCATION

Section 1. Superintendent of Public Instruction

The supervision of public instruction shall be vested in a state superintendent and such other officers as the legislature shall direct; and their qualifications, powers, duties and compensation shall be prescribed by law. The state superintendent shall be chosen by the qualified electors of the state at the same time and in the same manner as members of the supreme court, and shall hold office for 4 years from the succeeding first Monday in July. The term of office, time and manner of electing or appointing all other officers of supervision of public instruction shall be fixed by law.

Section 2. School Fund Created; Income Applied

The proceeds of all lands that have been or hereafter may be granted by the United States to this state for educational purposes (except the lands heretofore granted for the purposes of a university) and all moneys and the clear proceeds of all property that may accrue to the state by forfeiture or escheat; and the clear proceeds of all fines collected in the several counties for any breach of the penal laws, and all moneys arising from any grant to the state where the purposes of such grant are not specified, and the 500,000 acres of land to which the state is entitled by the provisions of an act of congress, entitled "An act to appropriate the proceeds of the sales of the public lands and to grant preemption rights," approved September 4, 1841; and also the 5 percent of the net proceeds of the public lands to which the state shall become entitled on admission into the union (if congress shall consent to such appropriation of the 2 grants last mentioned) shall be set apart as a separate fund to be called "the school fund," the interest of which and all other revenues derived from the school lands shall be exclusively applied to the following objects, to wit:

(1) To the support and maintenance of common schools, in each school district, and the purchase of suitable libraries and apparatus therefore.

(2) The residue shall be appropriated to the support and maintenance of academies and normal schools and suitable libraries and apparatus therefore.

Section 3. District Schools; Tuition; Sectarian Instruction; Released Time

The legislature shall provide by law for the establishment of district schools, which shall be as nearly uniform as practicable; and such schools shall be free and without charge for tuition to all children between the ages of 4 and 20 years; and no sectarian instruction shall be allowed therein; but the legislature by law may, for the purpose of religious instruction outside the district schools, authorize the release of students during regular school hours.

Section 4. Annual School Tax

Each town and city shall be required to raise by tax, annually, for the support of common schools therein, a sum not less than one-half the amount received by such town or city respectively for school purposes from the income of the school fund.

Section 5. Income of School Fund

Provision shall be made by law for the distribution of the income of the school fund among the several towns and cities of the state for the support of common schools therein, in some just proportion to the number of children and youth resident therein between the ages of four and twenty years, and no appropriation shall be made from the school fund to any city or town for the year in which said city or town shall fail to raise such tax; nor to any school district for the year in which a school shall not be maintained at least three months.

Section 6. State University; Support

Provision shall be made by law for the establishment of a state university at or near the seat of state government, and for connecting with the same, from time to time, such colleges in different parts of the state as the interests of education may require. The proceeds of all lands that have been or may hereafter be granted by the United States to the state for the support of a university shall be and remain a perpetual fund to be called "the university fund," the interest of which shall be appropriated to the support of the state university, and no sectarian instruction shall be allowed in such university.

Section 7. Commissioners of Public Lands

The secretary of state, treasurer and attorney general, shall constitute a board of commissioners for the sale of the school and university lands and for the investment of the funds arising therefrom. Any two of said commissioners shall be a quorum for the transaction of all business pertaining to the duties of their office.

Section 8. Sale of Public Lands

Provision shall be made by law for the sale of all school and university lands after they shall have been appraised; and when any portion of such lands shall be sold and the purchase money shall not be paid at the time of the sale, the commissioners shall take security by mortgage upon the lands sold for the sum remaining unpaid, with seven per cent interest thereon, payable annually at the office of the treasurer. The commissioners shall be authorized to execute a good and sufficient conveyance to all purchasers of such lands, and to discharge any mortgages taken as security, when the sum due thereon shall have been paid. The commissioners shall have power to withhold from sale any portion of such lands when they shall deem it expedient, and shall invest all moneys arising from the sale of such lands, as well as all other university and school funds, in such manner as the legislature shall provide, and shall give such security for the faithful performance of their duties as may be required by law.

ARTICLE XI: CORPORATIONS

Section 1. Corporations; How Formed

Corporations without banking powers or privileges may be formed under general laws, but shall not be created by special act, except for municipal purposes. All general laws or special acts enacted under the provisions of this section may be altered or repealed by the legislature at any time after their passage.

Section 2. Property Taken by Municipality

No municipal corporation shall take private property for public use, against the consent of the owner, without the necessity thereof being first established in the manner prescribed by the legislature.

Section 3. Municipal Home Rule; Debt Limit; Tax to Pay Debt

(1) Cities and villages organized pursuant to state law may determine their local affairs and government, subject only to this constitution and to such enactments of the legislature of statewide concern as with uniformity shall affect every city or every village. The method of such determination shall be prescribed by the legislature.

(2) No county, city, town, village, school district, sewerage district or other municipal corporation may become indebted in an amount that exceeds an allowable percentage of the taxable property located therein equalized for state purposes as provided by the legislature. In all cases the allowable percentage shall be 5 percent except as specified in pars. (a) and (b):

(a) For any city authorized to issue bonds for school purposes, an additional 10 percent shall be permitted for school purposes only, and in such cases the territory attached to the city for school purposes shall be included in the total taxable property supporting the bonds issued for school purposes.

(b) For any school district which offers no less than grades one to 12 and which at the time of incurring such debt is eligible for the highest level of school aids, 10 percent shall be permitted.

(3) Any county, city, town, village, school district, sewerage district or other municipal corporation incurring any indebtedness under sub. (2) shall, before or at the time of doing so, provide for the collection of a direct annual tax sufficient to pay the interest on such debt as it falls due, and also to pay and discharge the principal thereof within 20 years from the time of contracting the same.

(4) When indebtedness under sub. (2) is incurred in the acquisition of lands by cities, or by counties or sewerage districts having a population of 150,000 or over, for public, municipal purposes, or for the permanent improvement thereof, or to purchase, acquire, construct, extend, add to or improve a sewage collection or treatment system which services all or a part of such city or county, the city, county or sewerage district incurring the indebtedness shall, before or at the time of so doing, provide for the collection of a direct annual tax sufficient to pay the interest on such debt as it falls due, and also to pay and discharge the principal thereof within a period not exceeding 50 years from the time of contracting the same.

(5) An indebtedness created for the purpose of purchasing, acquiring, leasing, constructing, extending, adding to, improving, conducting, controlling, operating or managing a public utility of a town, village, city or special district, and secured solely by the property or income of such public utility, and whereby no municipal liability is created, shall not be considered an indebtedness of such town, village, city or special district, and shall not be included in arriving at the debt limitation under sub. (2).

Section 3a. Acquisition of Lands by State and Subdivisions; Sale of Excess

The state or any of its counties, cities, towns or villages may acquire by gift, dedication, purchase, or condemnation lands for establishing, laying out, widening, enlarging, extending, and maintaining memorial grounds, streets, highways, squares, parkways, boulevards, parks, playgrounds, sites for public buildings, and reservations in and about and along and leading to any or all of the same; and after the establishment, layout, and completion of such improvements, may convey any such real estate thus acquired and not necessary for such improvements, with reservations concerning the future use and occupation of such real estate, so as to protect such public works and improvements, and their environs, and to preserve the view, appearance, light, air, and usefulness of such public works. If the governing body of a county, city, town or village elects to accept a gift or dedication of land made on condition that the land be devoted to a special purpose and the condition subsequently becomes impossible or impracticable, such governing body may by resolution or ordinance enacted by a two-thirds vote of its members elect either to grant the land back to the donor or dedicator or his heirs or accept from the donor or dedicator or his heirs a grant relieving the county, city, town or village of the condition; however, if the donor or dedicator or his heirs are unknown or cannot be found, such resolution or ordinance may provide for the commencement of proceedings in the manner and in the courts as the legislature shall designate for the purpose of relieving the county, city, town or village from the condition of the gift or dedication.

Section 4. General Banking Law

The legislature may enact a general banking law for the creation of banks, and for the regulation and supervision of the banking business.

Section 5.

Repealed

ARTICLE XII: AMENDMENTS

Section 1. Constitutional Amendments

Any amendment or amendments to this constitution may be proposed in either house of the legislature, and if the same shall be agreed to by a majority of the members elected to each of the two houses, such proposed amendment or amendments shall be entered on their journals, with the yeas and nays taken thereon, and referred to the legislature to be chosen at the next general election, and shall be published for three months previous to the time of holding such election; and if, in the legislature so next chosen, such proposed amendment or amendments shall be agreed to by a majority of all the members elected to each house, then it shall be the duty of the legislature to submit such proposed amendment or amendments to the people in such manner and at such time as the legislature shall prescribe; and if the people shall approve and ratify such amendment or amendments by a majority of the electors voting thereon, such amendment or amendments shall become part of the constitution; provided, that if more than one amendment be submitted, they shall be submitted in such manner that the people may vote for or against such amendments separately.

Section 2. Constitutional Conventions

If at any time a majority of the senate and assembly shall deem it necessary to call a convention to revise or change this constitution, they shall recommend to the electors to vote for or against a convention at the next election for members of the legislature. And if it shall appear that a majority of the electors voting thereon have voted for a convention, the legislature shall, at its next session, provide for calling such convention.

ARTICLE XIII: MISCELLANEOUS PROVISIONS

Section 1. Political Year; Elections

The political year for this state shall commence on the first Monday of January in each year, and the general election shall be held on the Tuesday next succeeding the first Monday of November in even-numbered years.

Section 2. Dueling

Repealed

Section 3. Eligibility to Office

(1) No member of congress and no person holding any office of profit or trust under the United States except postmaster, or under any foreign power, shall be eligible to any office of trust, profit or honor in this state.

(2) No person convicted of a felony, in any court within the United States, no person convicted in federal court of a crime designated, at the time of commission, under federal law as a misdemeanor involving a violation of public trust and no person convicted, in a court of a state, of a crime designated, at the time of commission, under the law of the state as a misdemeanor involving a violation of public trust shall be eligible to any office of trust, profit or honor in this state unless pardoned of the conviction.

(3) No person may seek to have placed on any ballot for a state or local elective office in this state the name of a person convicted of a felony, in any court within the United States, the name of a person convicted in federal court of a crime designated, at the time of commission, under federal law as a misdemeanor involving a violation of public trust or the name of a person convicted, in a court of a state, of a crime designated, at the time of commission, under the law of the state as a misdemeanor involving a violation of public trust, unless the person named for the ballot has been pardoned of the conviction.

Section 4. Great Seal

It shall be the duty of the legislature to provide a great seal for the state, which shall be kept by the secretary of state, and all official acts of the governor, his approbation of the laws excepted, shall be thereby authenticated.

Section 5. Residents on Indian Lands, Where to Vote

Repealed

Section 6. Legislative Officers

The elective officers of the legislature, other than the presiding officers, shall be a chief clerk and a sergeant at arms, to be elected by each house.

Section 7. Division of Counties

No county with an area of nine hundred square miles or less shall be divided or have any part stricken therefrom, without submitting the question to a vote of the people of the county, nor unless a majority of all the legal voters of the county voting on the question shall vote for the same.

Section 8. Removal of County Seats

No county seat shall be removed until the point to which it is proposed to be removed shall be fixed by law, and a majority of the voters of the county voting on the question shall have voted in favor of its removal to such point.

Section 9. Election or Appointment of Statutory Officers

All county officers whose election or appointment is not provided for by this constitution shall be elected by the electors of the respective counties, or appointed by the boards of supervisors, or other county authorities, as the legislature shall direct. All city, town and village officers whose election or appointment is not provided for by this constitution shall be elected by the electors of such cities, towns and villages, or of some division thereof, or appointed by such authorities thereof as the legislature shall designate for that purpose. All other officers whose election or appointment is not provided for by this constitution, and all officers whose offices may hereafter be created by law, shall be elected by the people or appointed, as the legislature may direct.

Section 10. Vacancies in Office

(1) The legislature may declare the cases in which any office shall be deemed vacant, and also the manner of filling the vacancy, where no provision is made for that purpose in this constitution.

(2) Whenever there is a vacancy in the office of lieutenant governor, the governor shall nominate a successor to serve for the balance of the unexpired term, who shall take office after confirmation by the senate and by the assembly.

Section 11. Passes, Franks and Privileges

No person, association, copartnership, or corporation, shall promise, offer or give, for any purpose, to any political committee, or any member or employee thereof, to any candidate for, or incumbent of any office or position under the constitution or laws, or under any ordinance of any town or municipality, of this state, or to any person at the request or for the advantage of all or any of them, any free pass or frank, or any privilege withheld from any person, for the traveling accommodation or transportation of any person or property, or the transmission of any message or communication.

Section 12. Recall of Elective Officers

The qualified electors of the state, of any congressional, judicial or legislative district or of any county may petition for the recall of any incumbent elective officer after the first year of the term for which the incumbent was elected, by filing a petition with the filing officer with whom the nomination petition to the office in the primary is filed, demanding the recall of the incumbent.

(1) The recall petition shall be signed by electors equaling at least twenty-five percent of the vote cast for the office of governor at the last preceding election, in the state, county or district which the incumbent represents.

(2) The filing officer with whom the recall petition is filed shall call a recall election for the Tuesday of the 6th week after the date of filing the petition or, if that Tuesday is a legal holiday, on the first day after that Tuesday which is not a legal holiday.

(3) The incumbent shall continue to perform the duties of the office until the recall election results are officially declared.

(4) Unless the incumbent declines within 10 days after the filing of the petition, the incumbent shall without filing be deemed to have filed for the recall election. Other candidates may file for the office in the manner provided by law for special elections. For the purpose of conducting elections under this section:

(a) When more than 2 persons compete for a nonpartisan office, a recall primary shall be held. The 2 persons receiving the highest number of votes in the recall primary shall be the 2 candidates in the recall election, except that if any candidate receives a majority of the total number of votes cast in the recall primary, that candidate shall assume the office for the remainder of the term and a recall election shall not be held.

(b) For any partisan office, a recall primary shall be held for each political party which is by law entitled to a separate ballot and from which more than one candidate competes for the party's nomination in the recall election. The person receiving the highest number of votes in the recall primary for each political party shall be that party's candidate in the recall election. Independent candidates and candidates representing political parties not entitled by law to a separate ballot shall be shown on the ballot for the recall election only.

(c) When a recall primary is required, the date specified under sub. (2) shall be the date of the recall primary and the recall election shall be held on the Tuesday of the 4th week after the recall primary or, if that Tuesday is a legal holiday, on the first day after that Tuesday which is not a legal holiday.

(5) The person who receives the highest number of votes in the recall election shall be elected for the remainder of the term.

(6) After one such petition and recall election, no further recall petition shall be filed against the same officer during the term for which he was elected.

(7) This section shall be self-executing and mandatory. Laws may be enacted to facilitate its operation but no law shall be enacted to hamper, restrict or impair the right of recall.

Section 13. Marriage

Only a marriage between one man and one woman shall be valid or recognized as a marriage in this state. A legal status identical or substantially similar to that of marriage for unmarried individuals shall not be valid or recognized in this state.

SCHEDULE

Section 1. Effect of Change from Territory to State

That no inconvenience may arise by reason of a change from a territorial to a permanent state government, it is declared that all rights, actions, prosecutions, judgments, claims and contracts, as well of individuals as of bodies corporate, shall continue as if no such change had taken place; and all process which may be issued under the authority of the territory of Wisconsin previous to its admission into the union of the United States shall be as valid as if issued in the name of the state.

Section 2. Territorial Laws Continued
All laws now in force in the territory of Wisconsin which are not repugnant to this constitution shall remain in force until they expire by their own limitation or be altered or repealed by the legislature.

Section 3. Territorial Fines Accrue to State

Repealed

Section 4. Rights of Action and Prosecutions Saved

Repealed

Section 5. Existing Officers Hold over

Repealed

Section 6. Seat of Government

Repealed

Section 7. Local Officers Hold over

Repealed

Section 8. Copy of Constitution for President

Repealed

Section 9. Ratification of Constitution; Election of Officers

Repealed

Section 10. Congressional Apportionment

Repealed

Section 11. First Elections

Repealed

Section 12. Legislative Apportionment

Repealed

Section 13. Common Law Continued in Force

Such parts of the common law as are now in force in the territory of Wisconsin, not inconsistent with this constitution, shall be and continue part of the law of this state until altered or suspended by the legislature.

Section 14. Officers, When to Enter on Duties

Repealed

Section 15. Oath of Office

Repealed

Section 16. Implementing Revised Structure of Judicial Branch

The terms of office of justices of the supreme court serving on August 1, 1978, shall expire on the July 31 next preceding the first Monday in January on which such terms would otherwise have expired, but such advancement of the date of term expiration shall not impair any retirement rights vested in any such justice if the term had expired on the first Monday in January.

www.ingramcontent.com/pod-product-compliance
Lightning Source LLC
Chambersburg PA
CBHW071419220526
45469CB00004B/1350